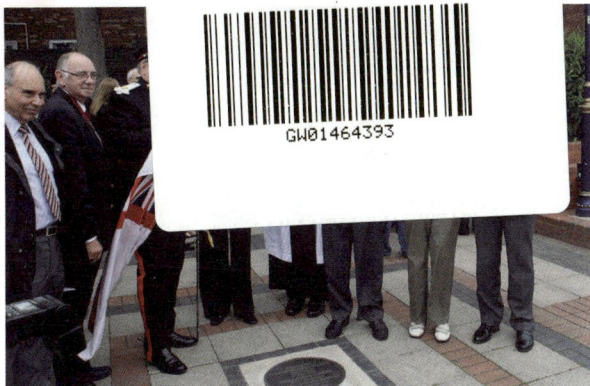

The Plaque Scheme, now closed, has been a remarkable example of collaborative working between participating societies and many others.

To keep costs to a minimum the Group offered a free service from inception to completion, covering research, design, permissions where necessary, ordering and fixing. That service also included arranging twenty-seven formal unveilings, often involving the Mayors of Broxtowe and Stapleford, dignitaries and family members. Others were fixed without ceremony at the request of property owners.

Plaques were cast from recycled aluminium and enamelled. An exception - Admiral Sir John Borlase Warren - was cast in bronze so that it could be set into the Walter Parker VC Memorial Square in Stapleford. All were prepared to designs based on English Heritage guidance by Leander Architectural of Dove Holes, Derbyshire, and became the responsibility of the property owner once fixed. Most are circular with a diameter between about 300mm (12") and 460mm (18").

Each subject was treated as a separate self-financed project, supported by small donations from owners, families and other interested parties to cover individual plaque costs only. Costs of supplying and fixing the plaques were covered in this way. This Guide, written and produced by Group members, was sponsored as a separate project.

Eleven of the plaques are within designated conservation areas (plaques 14, 15, 16, 17, 22, 23, 25, 27, 30, 33, 34), and nine required listed building consent, that is they are associated directly with a building of architectural or historic interest (plaques 1, 2, 6, 9, 15, 16, 27, 31, 32).

THE SIX TOWNSHIPS

LOCATION DETAILS

Plaques are listed by township in a clockwise direction, with precise location details shown at the foot of each page, including postal address, postcode, and a National Grid Reference (NGR) number. Unveiling and fixing dates are also shown for interest. There is a more detailed fold-out map at the back.

An Illustrated Guide To The Blue Plaques

Of Beeston, Chilwell, Attenborough, Toton, Stapleford & Bramcote

General
HENRY IRETON
Lawyer, confederate
and son-in-law
of Oliver Cromwell
born here 1611
died Limerick 1651

WILLIAM THOMPSON (BENDIGO)
1811-1880
All-England champion
bare-knuckle prize-fighter
reformed drunkard
turned evangelist
retired to a cottage
on this site

THE CHILWELL EXPLOSION
On 1st July 1918 an explosion
destroyed part of the
Chilwell Shell Filling Factory
killing 139 workers.

Many of the victims are
buried in these graves.

CONTENTS

INTRODUCTION

Sitting on the county boundary between Nottinghamshire and Derbyshire are the townships of Beeston, Chilwell, Attenborough, Toton, Stapleford and Bramcote - all in the south of Broxtowe, an area rich in history. A borough since 1977, Broxtowe is part of one of Nottinghamshire's ancient 'Hundreds' dating back to Saxon times.

These six townships were home to some quite extraordinary individuals from the past. Innovators, industrialists and entrepreneurs, figures from the worlds of journalism, banking, stage and screen, sport, science, the church and the military have all left their mark. Our plaques are a reminder of the links between the people who have shaped our community and the places where they lived and worked. They celebrate achievement with a local flavour.

Transport pioneer, Thomas Barton, was the first to be commemorated on 25th August 2010, with Beeston Station - the last of thirty-four - unveiled on 8th October 2014. Sir Neil Cossons, the Beeston-born Chairman of English Heritage from 2000-2007, attended both ceremonies.

The plaques and this Guide are essentially the work of seven volunteers from four local societies. We came together in 2009 as a partnership to identify, select and research the people and places that have shaped our local communities, with the clear objectives of marking achievement and place.

This was an ambitious task. There were ground rules to be set and decisions made about whom to celebrate and research. Judgements were needed about appropriateness and quality of information. Many issues, such as the spread and possible concentrations of subjects needed care and always there were the practicalities of funding to manage. Inevitably we have not been able to respond to every suggestion, leaving opportunities for others to add their own contributions in time.

Southern Broxtowe is special because of the rich legacy we have inherited. By pooling resources we have been able to be more thorough in shedding light on our common past and, perhaps, we can also help to inform the future with a little more understanding and care.

Southern Broxtowe Blue Plaque Group
Spring 2016

The Southern Broxtowe Blue Plaque Group has its origins in an English Heritage initiative to encourage marking achievement in the East Midlands going back to 2005.

The thirty-four plaques are the product of a collaboration driven by representatives from the Beeston and District Civic Society, the Beeston & District Local History Society, the Stapleford and District Local History Society, and the Bramcote Conservation Society.

Our focus has been on the communities of Beeston, Chilwell, Attenborough, Toton, Stapleford and Bramcote, where the participating societies are active. For much of this period of partnership from 2009, the Group representatives were:

- **Barbara Brooke**
  Stapleford and District Local History Society

- **Alan Clayton**
  Beeston & District Local History Society

- **Alan Dance**
  Beeston & District Local History Society

- **Peter Hillier**
  Bramcote Conservation Society

- **Robin Phillips**
  Beeston and District Civic Society

- **Peter Robinson** (Chair)
  Beeston and District Civic Society

- **Stephen Wallwork**
  Beeston and District Civic Society
  and Beeston & District Local History Society

FRANCIS WILKINSON
1844-1897

One of Beeston's greatest 19th century entrepreneurs and better known as Frank, this was the man behind the flamboyant Anglo Scotian Mills building, now the Lace Mill. Born in Hucknall, the son of a framework knitter, he moved with his family to Chilwell, setting up first as a shawl maker and later as a net-curtain manufacturer, with his purpose-built Anglo Scotian Mills in Beeston becoming Europe's biggest net-curtain factory.

> **FRANCIS WILKINSON**
> 1844 - 1897
> Re-built
> Anglo Scotian Mills 1892
> then the largest
> net curtain factory
> in Europe

Anglo Scotian Mills, courtesy of C P Walker

Frank quickly established a reputation for quality and good value in Britain and built a thriving export trade to North America, where his quality net curtains were in great demand. On one occasion he hired a special train from Beeston to the docks to transport a large New York order.

The works were swiftly rebuilt after fires in 1886 and 1892, and after the American imposition of tariffs on imported lace in 1890 he also moved quickly to manufacture in the USA. Unfortunately, career success was cut short by his premature death at the age of fifty-three. *The Beeston Times* reported that *'Beeston has lost one of the best friends it ever had.'* His older brother George succeeded him and briefly continued the business **(plaque 12)**.

The imposing 1892 structure and Albion Street buildings are Grade II listed.

Francis Mill, Albion Street, Beeston, NG9 2UZ
NGR: SK 5275 3714
Plaque fixed 26th August 2012

WILLIAM THOMPSON (BENDIGO)
1811-1880

The renowned bare-knuckle prize-fighter, born in Nottingham, claimed to be one of triplets and the youngest of twenty-one children. However, records show that he was one of twins and the fifth of only six children.

WILLIAM THOMPSON (BENDIGO)
1811-1880
All-England champion bare-knuckle prize-fighter reformed drunkard turned evangelist retired to a cottage on this site

Bendigo secured a job with an iron turner in 1828, about the time that he took up boxing. Between 1832 and 1850 he fought twenty prizefights, losing only once, and became All-England Champion. But drink was his weakness. He was sent to the House of Correction some twenty-eight times for being drunk and disorderly.

Bendigo in fighting pose

In 1873 Bendigo heard the evangelist Dick Weaver preach at the Nottingham Mechanics Institute. Inspired, he renounced drink to become an evangelist himself.

The following year he moved to one of a row of cottages, now demolished, next to the Lace Mill on Wollaton Road, Beeston – possibly the end cottage marked by a tall domestic chimney built into the mill wall. Bendigo was injured when fishing by the Trent at Beeston in early July 1880, and was taken home to recover. He suffered further injury that led to his death in August, when he fell downstairs.

Buried in St Mary's burial ground in Bath Street, Nottingham, Bendigo remains one of England's greatest bare-knuckle fighters. The City of Greater Bendigo in Victoria, Australia, bears his name.

The Lace Mill,
92 Wollaton Road,
Beeston, NG9 2NN
NGR: SK 5267 3714
Plaque unveiled
11th October 2011

Bendigo in old age

SITE OF SWISS MILLS
1886-1984

The Swiss Mills owed their origin to the Pollards, one of Beeston's great lace-making families. John Pollard (1838-1903) added the Wollaton Road building to a group of older works in the Cross Street/Villa Street area in 1886. John was the second of four generations of the Pollard family – Thomas, John, Arthur and John – that made lace on this site from the 1840s until 1953. They started modestly with hand-operated machines, gradually embracing steam power.

Swiss Mills with John Pollard Junior, 1950s, courtesy of Ernest Pollard

When lace demand was high, the machines worked from 4am until midnight, reputedly causing the building to sway.

The plain Swiss Mills stood in contrast to its Anglo Scotian Mills neighbour, reflecting the characters of the men who built them – the practical, earthy John Pollard and the flamboyant Frank Wilkinson **(plaque 1)**.

The Pollard business, noted for fine quality Leavers lace, peaked in the early 20th century. A clock and belfry, incorporating The Ten Bell **(plaque 4)** were added in 1903, and in 1909 Pollards bought Anglo Scotian Mills. Arthur Pollard, regarded in Nottingham as the most gifted lace man of his time, died in 1952. His son John oversaw the end of lace making by the family in Beeston shortly afterwards.

A spectacular fire on 29th March 1984 finally destroyed a landmark and the legacy of one of Beeston's most successful lace families. The origin of the name Swiss Mills is currently a mystery.

46 Wollaton Road, Beeston, NG9 2NR
NGR: SK 5276 3703
Plaque unveiled 27th May 2014

THE TEN BELL
1841

Passers-by might wonder why there is a bronze bell in Sainsbury's Stoney Street forecourt.

THE TEN BELL
1841
Hung at Beeston Silk Mill and rung ten minutes before half-day school for child workers
Moved to Swiss Mills in 1903

The story goes back to the Factory Acts of 1833 and 1844, limiting working hours for children aged nine to thirteen, and imposing a minimum level of schooling. In response, some factory owners devised a shift system so that older workers had children to help them throughout their longer working day.

Swiss Mills before 1984 fire, courtesy of David Hallam

In 1841, this bell was installed on the Silk Mill on the eastern corner of High Road and Station Road. There it rang at ten to nine, calling the children of the afternoon shift to the mill school, and at ten to two, calling children working the morning shift. So it became known as The Ten Bell. It was also used to call out the local fire brigade from time to time.

After the Silk Mill closed in 1902, the bell was transferred the following year to the roof of the Swiss Mills on Wollaton Road **(plaque 3)**, remaining there until 1983 when it was acquired by Broxtowe Borough Council. Fortunately, the bell was removed a few months before the Swiss Mills fire of March 1984, and shortly afterwards was made a feature of the Sainsbury development.

Stoney Street, Beeston, NG9 2LA

NGR: SK 5291 3706

Plaque unveiled 11th September 2014

Former Silk Mill from Square, late 1930s

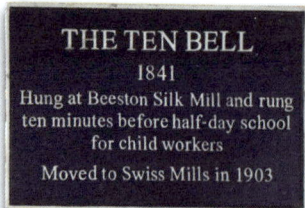

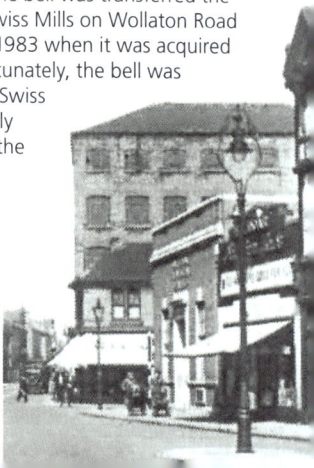

SIR LOUIS FREDERICK PEARSON, CBE
1863-1943

Pearson was a family synonymous with the area's industrial heritage for over 200 years, from nurseries to horticultural buildings and foundries.

Sir LOUIS FREDERICK PEARSON CBE
1863 - 1943
Co-founder of Beeston Foundry Co later Beeston Boiler Co gave this park in 1923 as a recreation ground to the people of Beeston

Louis Frederick Pearson was the great-grandson of nurseryman John Pearson **(plaque 20)** and the youngest brother of Henry John Pearson **(plaque 34)** and with him founded the Beeston Foundry Company in 1893, later the Beeston Boiler Company. He became chairman after Henry's death, playing a significant part during WW1 when the company assisted with war production, and as chairman of Nottingham Munitions Board of Management, for which he was awarded the CBE in 1919. Post-war, the business developed further at home and abroad, and he was knighted in 1923.

Beeston Boiler Company, 1935

In 1889 he married Gertrude Potter with whom he had three children. Away from industry he was active in public life. In 1923 he presented the Broadgate Recreation Ground – at one time named after him – to the people of Beeston. He was a generous financial supporter of Nottingham General Hospital, its president in 1924-5 and chairman of the board for 1933-42. Sir Louis was appointed High Sheriff for Nottinghamshire for 1934. He served as a president of the Beeston Lads' Club and left behind an impressive industrial legacy. On his death he bequeathed his home, Lenton Grove, to the hospital.

Broadgate Park, Broadgate, Beeston, NG9 2LN
NGR: SK 5313 3716
Plaque unveiled
18th April 2013

Portrait in later life

EDWARD JOSEPH LOWE, FRS
1825-1900

A pioneering weather researcher, astronomer and eminent botanist, Edward Lowe was born at Highfield House (now within Nottingham University grounds), where his father Alfred Joseph Lowe (1789-1856) had an observatory.

EDWARD JOSEPH LOWE FRS
1825-1900
Astronomer, botanist a founder member of the Meteorological Society built Broadgate House as his residence and observatory

Edward began the first of a series of meteorological observations at the age of fifteen.
He was a meticulous weather observer; he provided daily weather information for *The Times*, wrote several papers and books, invented the dry powder test for ozone, was a founder member of the British (later Royal) Meteorological Society and as an astronomer he did particular research into meteors.

Lowe's Beeston 'Pepperpot' Observatory

Broadgate House (Grade II listed) was built by him as his home from 1851, and included an observatory on the roof to accommodate astronomical instruments, a feature still visible today. His father had already built a second observatory near Beeston Railway Station and known locally as 'The Pepperpot', but this was demolished c.1963.

As a renowned botanist Lowe was a leading authority on British and exotic ferns, on grasses and shells, and published many illustrated papers on them. He was a Fellow of many learned societies – Linnaean, Astronomical, Geological, Zoological and Horticultural and was honoured as a Fellow of the Royal Society (FRS) in 1867.

72 Broadgate, Beeston, NG9 2FW
NGR: SK 5340 3745
Plaque fixed 20th November 2011

Edward Joseph Lowe, FRS

THOMAS HUMBER
1841-1910

Thomas Humber is the man who brought industrial-scale cycle manufacturing to Beeston. A talented engineer, he worked in various small Nottingham businesses, until, inspired by a French velocipede, he set up to copy, improve and then manufacture cycles in his home workshop.

THOMAS HUMBER
1841 - 1910
Engineer
made bicycles
motorcycles and cars
here and later
in Coventry

Humber Cycle Works, c.1904, courtesy of Mr W Spencer and www.picturethepast.org.uk

Progressing to bigger premises, he moved his home and business to Beeston in 1878. He worked through two successive partnerships, formed a limited company in 1887, then built larger premises on New Lane – later renamed Humber Road – where the distinctive Humber 'Wheel of Life' symbols can still be seen on the surviving building.

Initially employing about eighty men, he continued to improve cycle design and workmanship quality. The company grew rapidly as sales and premises expanded and, although Thomas retired from active participation in 1892, by 1898 there were some 2,000 employees, making the company Beeston's largest employer and one of the country's major cycle firms.

The description 'Beeston Humber' became synonymous worldwide with quality and reliability, putting Beeston on the world cycle map. In the 1890s and beyond, bicycles and tricycles were favoured by royalty, some adverts proclaiming 'Humber, the Royal Cycle'.

HM King Edward VII on his Humber Tricycle

Manufacture of motorcycles began in 1896, followed shortly afterwards by motorcars. However, a decision was later made to move all manufacture to Coventry. The Beeston works closed in 1908, leaving hundreds of empty houses as families sought work elsewhere.

The Dojo, Humber Road, Beeston, NG9 2ET
NGR: SK 5356 3695
Plaque unveiled 21st August 2011

LT. COLONEL DR BRIAN DUNCAN SHAW, MM
1898-1999

Popularly known as 'BD' he was renowned locally and internationally for his noisy and hair-raising demonstration lectures on explosives. These started in 1930 at Nottingham University College, when, as a lecturer, Shaw was asked to improve the attendance at the Student Chemical and Physical Society meetings. By 1990, he had given this lively lecture over 1,600 times, including for BBC TV. When he finally left his Beeston home, the bomb squad was called to check it for safety!

Lt Colonel
Dr BRIAN DUNCAN
'BD' SHAW MM
1898-1999
Organic chemist, popular lecturer on explosives, distinguished marksman and war hero lived here

Explosives Lecture, 1966

BD was a skilled marksman and fought in both World Wars, reaching the rank of Lt. Colonel. In WW1 he fought at the Somme, Cambrai and Passchendaele and received the Military Medal for bravery near Cambrai in 1917. During WW2, in command of the 1/5th Battalion Sherwood Foresters, he was left behind after the evacuation from Dunkirk in 1940, was taken prisoner, escaped, but was recaptured. After his release in 1945 he returned to the University, retaining a military role as CO of the University Officer Training Corps.

He was a frequent competitor at Bisley, winning many shooting trophies over the years. He died aged 101, not quite achieving his ambition to span three centuries.

**185 Queen's Road,
Beeston, NG9 2FE**

NGR: SK 5350 3675

**Plaque fixed
16th November 2012**

*Lt. Colonel
Dr B D Shaw,
1950*

BEESTON STATION
Opened 1839

Beeston is the only station on the Nottingham to Derby line to have remained continuously on the same site since being opened to the public by the Midland Counties Railway on 4th June 1839. The company's other route, from Trent Junction to Leicester and Rugby, opened in 1840.

Midland
Counties Railway
Surveyed by Charles B Vignoles

BEESTON STATION
Opened 4th June 1839

Rebuilt by the
Midland Railway 1847
Refurbished by British Rail
1988

The surveyor of the line was Charles B Vignoles, an eminent railway engineer who had developed the use of the flat-bottom rail. The Midland Counties forbade him to employ it on their lines, but it is now used, very successfully, worldwide.

In 1844, the Midland Counties Railway, the Birmingham and Derby Junction Railway and the North Midland Railway, amalgamated to form the Midland Railway. In 1847 this company replaced Beeston's original small station building with the one still in use today.

Beeston Station, c.1904, courtesy of Mr W Spencer and www.picturethepast.org.uk

With the 1923 grouping of Britain's railways, the Midland Railway became a part of the London, Midland and Scottish Railway, until nationalisation in 1948. Beeston Station achieved Grade II listing in 1987. In 1988, having fallen into a very poor state of repair, British Rail sympathetically restored the building to its Victorian splendour.

Station Road, Beeston, NG9 1JU

NGR: SK 5338 3623

Plaque unveiled 8th October 2014

Beeston Station, 1839
R. Allen's Nottingham and Derby Railway Companion

WILLIAM FREDERICK WALLETT
1813-1892

Actor and entertainer, Wallett styled himself 'The Queen's Jester' after a performance on 19th July 1844 at Windsor Castle for Queen Victoria and Prince Albert and a large party of distinguished guests, including the Duke of Wellington. Wallett was received kindly, but his self-styled title had no official royal authority.

WILLIAM FREDERICK WALLETT (THE QUEEN'S JESTER) 1813 - 1892 International circus and stage entertainer Moved to Beeston in 1862 lived here from 1879

Wallett in later life

Born in Hull, he was the oldest of five boys and two girls. His career as a circus performer and entertainer in music halls and light theatres spanned sixty years, both in Britain and in the USA. A man of striking ability and versatility, often performing in Court Jester's costume, he delighted audiences with his original wit and humour. A feeling for popular taste and a skill for self-promotion kept him in demand well into later life. His posters proclaimed *'Wallett is here!'*

Wallett was married to Mary Orme, the daughter of a Hull publican, from 1839 until her death in 1861. Beeston became his base shortly after his second marriage in 1862 to Sarah Farmer of the Nottingham entertainment family, and in 1879 they moved to Station Road.

An amusing raconteur, witty, charming and compassionate, he died at his Beeston home in 1892. A memorial survives in Nottingham General Cemetery.

220 Station Road, Beeston, NG9 2AA
NGR: SK 5324 3637
Plaque unveiled 12th February 2013

Wallett in Court Jester's costume

REV. DR JOHN CLIFFORD, CH
1836-1923

John Clifford rose from humble beginnings to become an eminent national leader of the Baptist denomination. Born at nearby Sawley, at the age of four he moved with his family to Beeston, where they worshipped at Nether Street Baptist Chapel (built 1806). He left school aged ten, working first in a local lace factory then for a year at Pearson's nursery gardens, Chilwell, before returning to lace factory life.

Rev Dr
JOHN CLIFFORD
CH
1836-1923
was baptised and preached
his first sermon here
Baptist Union President
Life-long opponent of
sectarian bias
in schooling

General Baptist Chapel, c.1900

John was baptised at Nether Street in 1851 and soon became a preacher, his first sermon being delivered there in 1855. Leaving Beeston, he trained at the Baptist Academy, Leicester. Then began a brilliant career in London, first as minister of Praed Street Baptist Chapel in Paddington, then later of nearby Westbourne Park Chapel, remaining there as minister for fifty-seven years. An eloquent speaker, social reformer and opponent of sectarian bias in schooling, he became President of the London Baptist Association in 1879, the Baptist Union in 1888 and 1899, and the Evangelical Free Church Council in 1898. He was appointed a Companion of Honour (CH) in the 1921 New Year Honours List, one of the first to receive this accolade.

Non-denominational education was his main concern, so it was very appropriate that he opened the school that bears his name on Nether Street in 1898.

Church House Nursery,
Nether Street, NG9 2AT
NGR: SK 5305 3664
Plaque unveiled
20th September 2011

Rev. Dr John Clifford

GEORGE WILKINSON
1841-1919

The builder of much of central Beeston's Victorian housing, George was born in Hucknall, an older brother of Frank, founder of the Anglo Scotian Mills **(plaque 1)**. George had a shawl-making business in Hucknall and took an interest in public affairs by serving on the Local Board until 1878. Later he was elected to the Beeston Local Board, becoming Chairman of the Urban District Council for two years from 1899, and also serving as a Nottinghamshire County Councillor from 1888.

The
White House
rebuilt 1910 by
GEORGE WILKINSON
1841 - 1919
Manager of Anglo-Scotian Mills
after the death of his
younger brother
Francis Wilkinson
in 1897

Derby Street and George Wilkinson

George managed Anglo Scotian Mills following Frank's death in 1897, but property was his principal legacy. He built many houses on streets that still survive, including Wilkinson Street, Commercial Avenue, Willoughby Street, Derby Street, City Road and Nether Street. He bought 45 Nether Street in 1895 and improved it for family occupation in 1910. It remains in Wilkinson family ownership to this day.

Anglo Scotian Mills ran into financial difficulties in the early 1900s, eventually to be bought from liquidators by the Pollard family, owners of the nearby Swiss Mills **(plaque 3)**. Lace and hosiery manufacture continued there until the 1960s. The imposing Wollaton Road building and that in Albion Street are Grade II listed and in recent years have been converted into apartments.

Courtesy of C P Walker

43 Nether Street, Beeston, NG9 2AT

NGR: SK 5322 3684

Plaque unveiled 31st October 2013

BEESTON LADS' CLUB
1913-2007

'Sure and Steadfast', like the Boys' Brigade motto, the club served the community in Station Road from 1913 to 2007, initially through the dedicated efforts of Stephen Hetley Pearson (1882-1917), and then by others who followed him.

BEESTON LADS' CLUB stood on this site 1913-2007 Founded in 1908 by **STEPHEN HETLEY PEARSON** who donated the building

Hetley, as he was more commonly known, began forming the club around 1908. Under his leadership numbers grew, funds were raised and factory premises on Station Road acquired and altered. Boys' Brigade founder, Sir William Smith, opened the building on 11th October 1913 and for ninety-four years doors were open to young men (and from 1974 to young women) seven days a week. Over the years many Beeston lads and lasses met the love of their lives at Lads' Club dances.

Beeston Lads' Club, courtesy of Neville Bostock

Involved in the brigade from 1899, Hetley was Captain of the 17th Nottingham (Beeston) Company, 1909-1917, by then the second largest brigade in the country. Son of Henry John Pearson **(plaque 34)**, Hetley trained as an accountant, becoming a director of the Beeston Foundry Company in 1907.

As a second lieutenant, 2nd Battalion Grenadier Guards, Hetley was killed on 1st December 1917 leading his men at the battle of Cambrai. He was one of forty Beeston Lads' Club old boys who died serving their country in WW1. His name and legacy live on in the Pearson Centre, Nuart Road, Beeston.

Tesco, 1 Station Road, Beeston, NG9 2WJ
NGR: SK 5291 3684
Plaque unveiled 7th November 2012

Stephen Hetley Pearson

ARTHUR COSSONS
1893-1963

An enthusiastic historian and pioneer in local history, Arthur Cossons was born in Somerset and grew up in Chippenham before starting work in 1907 in various outfitters' shops. In WW1 he enlisted in the Royal Army Medical Corps, serving at home and overseas.

ARTHUR COSSONS
1893 - 1963
Distinguished historian and author
Headmaster at Church Street
Junior Boys School
on this site
1932 - 1958

Church Street School and Arthur Cossons, 1950s

Back in civilian life, Arthur started training as a teacher, matriculating in 1921. In the following year he was appointed a teacher at Church Street Boys School, Beeston, and in 1930 as headmaster of Lenton Abbey Junior School (which was replaced by Beeston Fields Junior School in 1932). From 1932 to retirement in 1958 he was headmaster of Church Street Junior Boys School. His interest was clearly in history, but with a particular passion for local history and its teaching, mainly focused on the Beeston area. He set up a unique school museum of local finds, encouraging children to go on expeditions and contribute to the museum's collections.

He wrote prolifically for newspapers, popular and academic journals, and books. He had a special interest in turnpikes, writing *The Turnpike Roads of Nottinghamshire* in 1934 and following it with similar studies on five other counties. He was an untiring protagonist for adult education, a keen conservationist and for many years the Honorary Secretary of the Nottinghamshire Branch of the Historical Association; but, above all, in the words of his son Sir Neil Cossons, he was 'a natural teacher'.

Church Street, Beeston, NG9 1FY
NGR: SK 5283 3672
Plaque unveiled 7th May 2011

Arthur Cossons, 1939

VILLAGE CROSS

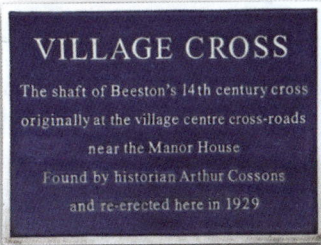

VILLAGE CROSS
The shaft of Beeston's 14th century cross originally at the village centre cross-roads near the Manor House
Found by historian Arthur Cossons and re-erected here in 1929

Also on Church Street, close to **plaque 14** and within the West End Conservation Area, this ancient stone possibly dates from the Middle Ages and is believed by some to be the shaft of Beeston's medieval village cross. It once stood near the present junction of Church Street, Dovecote Lane, West End **(plaque 17)** and Middle Street, close to where the war memorial now stands. Thus it was at the centre of the old village, with the Manor House **(plaque 16)** and parish church nearby.

Site of the cross, early 1900s

The cross was removed in the 1850s and was lost, but in 1929 the shaft was found embedded in a wall at Manor Lodge by historian Arthur Cossons **(plaque 14)**. As headmaster at Church Street Junior Boys School (demolished 2005), it was appropriate that he had it re-erected close to this school.

The village cross has sometimes been referred to as a market cross, as it is believed that a corn market was formerly held nearby. Middle Street, from the war memorial to Station Road (formerly Brown Lane), was known as Market Street until the late 1860s. The historical value of the shaft is recognised by its Grade II listing.

Church Street, Beeston, NG9 1FY
NGR: SK 5282 3674
Plaque unveiled 7th May 2011

Remaining shaft in 1976

BEESTON MANOR HOUSE

Situated on Middle Street, close to the heart of the old village, the Manor House is one of Beeston's oldest buildings, Grade II listed and within the Beeston West End Conservation Area. This part of Middle Street was called Market Street until the late 1860s – see **plaque 15** for more details.

BEESTON MANOR HOUSE

originally timber-framed rebuilt in brick c. 1675 and 1725 Home of the Strey family lords of the manor 16th - 19th centuries then home of the Venn family until 1978

Manor House from lawn

At the base of the wall of the house is a stone plinth that once carried a timber-framed building, home of the Beauchamp family, early Lords of the Manor. The parlour wing facing Middle Street was rebuilt in brick about 1725, following a rebuild of the south wing in about 1675. In the 1970s, rendering was removed, revealing the original brickwork, and decorative brickwork above the bricked-up windows was restored to indicate the original pattern.

From the 16th to the 19th century the Strey family held the Lordship, and when Richard Strey died in 1797 it passed to a cousin. The house was bought in 1840 by surgeon John Orton who gave it to his daughter Elizabeth when she married Benjamin Baker Venn in 1866 and it remained with the Venns, a family with lace making and hosiery interests, until 1978. So for almost 400 years, only two families occupied the Manor House.

2 Middle Street, Beeston, NG9 1FX

NGR: SK 5290 3663

Plaque fixed
26th August 2012

Middle Street with Manor House (white, left)
Elsie Woods, 1957, courtesy of Broxtowe Borough Council

WEST END

This short street in the Beeston West End Conservation Area boasts the largest concentration of listed buildings in Beeston – six in all.

They include 16th to 18th century former farmhouses which, together with the Manor House on Middle Street **(plaque 16)**, are Beeston's oldest houses, perhaps replacing even older buildings on the same sites. The oldest surviving, No. 6, West End House, dates from the 1560s and its occupants would have witnessed the deadly bubonic plague hitting Beeston in 1593. Centuries later its use changed from farmhouse to school, run first by Elizabeth Henshall in the late 19th century, followed briefly by Maud Mary Willett and then, for forty-four years up to 1947, by Miss Amy Eleanor Horner. Her name is still remembered by many.

No.6, West End House

No. 3, The Old Manor House, (not to be confused with the even older Middle Street Manor House), may be associated with a small Beeston manor owned by Wymondley Priory in Hertfordshire from the 12th to the 16th centuries.

In all, a street of prestigious buildings bearing out that the wealthiest houses in any community tended to lie west of the centre, since the prevailing wind blew chimney smoke towards the east.

1-3 West End,
Beeston, NG9 1GL
NGR: SK 5280 3654
Plaque fixed
5th November 2013

No.3, Old Manor House from the garden

SID STANDARD
1931-2003

Of national renown in cycling sport, Sid was greatly respected in the community, trading in Chilwell Road from 1973 to 2000. An inspirational figure, he introduced hundreds of young people to competitive and recreational cycling over fifty years, leading to the Beeston area acquiring a strong cycling reputation. The concentration of interest and talent has much to do with Sid's shop, started and run by Arthur Panter in 1927. Advice, equipment, service and enthusiasm offered by Arthur and Sid have been key ingredients to success.

SID STANDARD
1931 - 2003
Cycling enthusiast
Inspired youngsters from this shop for many years
'It's all rideable'

Plaque unveiling, 14th September 2014, courtesy of Alan Clayton

Some local riders achieved greatness at national and international level - Ray Booty who took a Commonwealth Games Gold in 1958, Olympic and Commonwealth Games medallists Ian Hallam in the 1970s and Bryan Steel in the early 21st century.

Sid died tragically in September 2003 while leading the junior section of the Cycling Touring Club on their weekly Sunday run. In tribute, 'Sid's Juniors' gather for a memorial ride, every year, close to the accident's anniversary. The plaque was unveiled on Sunday 14th September 2014 at the start of their eleventh anniversary run.

His motto to a life dedicated to cycling was that 'It's all rideable'.

A tram has been named in Sid's honour as a community hero.

35-37 Chilwell Road, Beeston, NG9 1EH
NGR: SK 5262 3654
Plaque unveiled
14th September 2014

Portrait, mid-1980s, courtesy of David Standard

T H BARTON, OBE (THE GUV'NOR)
1866-1946

T.H. BARTON
OBE
(THE GUV'NOR)
1866-1946
Engineer, inventor, innovator
Pioneer of motor bus transport

Worked here
1913-1946

A pioneer of the bus world, Thomas Henry Barton grew up in Derbyshire before moving on and serving a number of engineering apprenticeships. While working on the development of oil engines, he took a keen interest in motorised transport, buying an 11-seater wagonette in 1897 to carry passengers in Mablethorpe and later in Derbyshire.

Thomas Barton and chassis, c.1930, courtesy of Simon Barton

Barton's first bus service used a charabanc running from Long Eaton to the 1908 Nottingham Goose Fair. As his Chilwell-based company grew, he enlarged the fleet and proved to be both innovator and inventor by experimenting with modifications to engines and bodywork. In both world wars he adapted some buses to run on town gas. The 1930s saw new style vehicles, a great increase in routes and the launch of touring holidays in Britain and Europe.

T H Barton was held in high regard by his employees, who referred to him as 'The Guv'nor'. He was awarded an OBE in 1944 for services to the passenger transport industry. After his death his legacy lived on through the company's post-war expansion to become Britain's largest independent bus operator.

**61 High Road,
Chilwell, NG9 4AJ**

NGR: SK 5236 3628

**Plaque unveiled
25th August 2010**

Portrait, 1944

GEORGE HENRY HURT
1873-1934

George Henry Hurt founded his hand-frame knitting business in 1912, a bold move when a once extensive local industry was in steep decline. Nevertheless, The Shawl Factory, as it is now known, is over a century old and still going strong, while preserving some old traditions.

GEORGE HENRY HURT
1873-1934
started his hand-frame knitting business here in 1912

Originally this building was a SEED WAREHOUSE built c.1781 for JOHN PEARSON nurseryman

The company remains with the Hurt family, and until 1968 they routinely used hand-frames for production – some over 200 years old. Now, high-quality shawl production relies on modern machines. Many shawls are sold or gifted to celebrities and to royalty, including those worn by Prince George and Princess Charlotte on their first public appearances in 2013 and 2015. Working hand-frames can be seen in operation on open days.

Working hand-frames, courtesy of the Hurt family

The building dates from c.1781, built by John Pearson (c.1752–1824) as a seed warehouse for his expanding nursery business. At one time he owned England's biggest orchard for sweet apples. Later generations of the Pearson family made significant contributions to the area **(plaques 5, 13 and 34).**

The Shawl Factory,
65 High Road,
Chilwell, NG9 4AJ

NGR: SK 5234 3626

Plaque unveiled
30th May 2012

Back row, centre - George Henry Hurt, Sergeant, Robin Hoods, 1899-1902

RICHARD BECKINSALE
1947-1979

From local lad to one of the most memorable actors on TV screens in the 1970s, Richard Arthur Beckinsale was born in Carlton and moved with his family to Woodland Grove, Chilwell, in the 1950s.

RICHARD BECKINSALE
1947 - 1979
Actor
Star of *Porridge* and *Rising Damp*
Attended
College House Junior School
1954-58
Lived in Woodland Grove
Chilwell

He was educated locally at College House Junior School (1954-58), then at Alderman White Secondary Modern School. After leaving school aged fifteen he worked in the bus upholstery section of Barton Transport Ltd. **(plaque 19)** before studying drama at Clarendon College, Nottingham, subsequently gaining a place at the Royal Academy of Dramatic Art (RADA).

Star audience at the unveiling, courtesy of Nigel Brooks

His first professional acting role was at Crewe Repertory Theatre, and whilst working there he made his TV debut in *Coronation Street*. His first TV starring role was in the sitcom *The Lovers* opposite Paula Wilcox, followed by two of the most successful ever TV comedy series, *Rising Damp* with Leonard Rossiter and *Porridge* with Ronnie Barker. In 1965 he married his first wife Margaret Bradley with whom he had daughter Samantha, born 1966.

With his second wife, actress Judy Loe, he had a daughter Kate, born 1973 and now an international stage, TV and film star. Tragically, Richard died of a heart attack at the age of only thirty-one at his home in Sunningdale, Berks.

College House Junior School, Cator Lane, Chilwell, NG9 4BB
NGR: SK 5201 3618
Plaque unveiled 17th July 2013

Richard Beckinsale, courtesy of Judy Loe

CHILWELL HALL
1300-1933

Excavations between 2005 and 2011 suggested long occupation of the Hall site, possibly to pre-Roman times, with the first recorded building, the Martell Manor, dating from 1300. This passed by marriage in 1420 to Sir William Babington (Chief Justice of England 1423-1436), who rebuilt the house and chapel in 1421.

Site of
CHILWELL HALL
1300-1933

Home of the
CHARLTON FAMILY
Landowners, prominent
in local affairs
1620-1932

Chilwell Hall frontage, c.1920

Chilwell Hall is primarily associated with the Charlton family, initially Middlesex merchants traceable to John de Charleton, MP for the City of London in 1318. The family acquired estates in Derbyshire in the mid-16th century, settling in Chilwell around 1620. They rebuilt the house in 1652 and again in 1803.

Charltons were active in Derbyshire and Nottinghamshire for over 300 years, as landowners, in the military, and as magistrates. At least two were appointed High Sheriffs of Nottinghamshire. Caroline, daughter of one, helped save the Hall from Reform Bill rioters in October 1831.

It was the Shell Filling Factory, built partly on Charlton land in 1915, that led to the break-up of an estate of 1,200 acres that had covered much of Chilwell. The Hall was demolished in 1933 after the family moved to Croxall in Staffordshire, where the last of the line died in a fire in 1942. The brick boundary wall to the Hall, a greenhouse and some garden trees survive in the Chilwell Conservation Area.

214-218 High Road, Chilwell, NG9 5DB
NGR: SK 5183 3595
Plaque fixed 15th December 2013

Charlton family Coat of Arms, 1857

GREGORY'S ROSES

Gregory's Roses placed Chilwell firmly on the world map in the 1950s, 60s and 70s.

Former offices of the world famous Chilwell Mark
GREGORY'S ROSES
Established here 1897 by
CHARLES GREGORY
1867 - 1940
and continued by his son
CHARLES WALTER GREGORY
1908 - 1980

Charles Gregory (1867-1940), a nurseryman and florist specialising in roses, first started trading at the Old Close Nurseries on High Road, Chilwell and later in both Chilwell and Stapleford. His son Charles Walter Gregory (1908-1980) joined the firm in the mid-1920s, taking over after his father's death in 1940. Both were active and well respected in the community.

The nurseries built up a national and international reputation for their quality Chilwell Mark roses. Gregory's received many awards over the years, cultivating popular new rose varieties and exhibiting regularly at the Chelsea Flower Show and many other shows throughout the

Charles and Walter Gregory, courtesy of Rosemary McCarthy

country. In the 1960s Gregory's Roses was one of Britain's top three rose growers with the largest rose fields in the land. Both nurseries continued in parallel until Old Close was sold in the 1960s.

The plaque is mounted on the former offices of Gregory's Roses, originally the premises of The Old Sick Club, a friendly society established in 1771. Local historian Robert Mellors, writing in 1920, believed the building to date from 1812; it is within the Chilwell Conservation Area.

307 High Road, Chilwell, NG9 5DL

NGR: SK 5162 3580

Plaque unveiled 16th February 2013

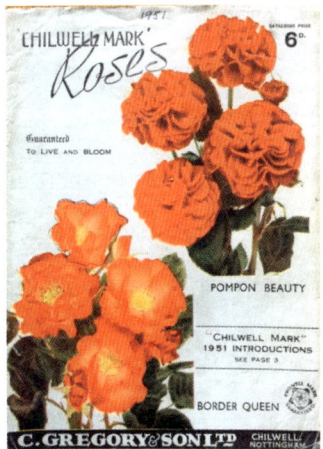

Advertisement, 1951, courtesy of Rosemary McCarthy

THE CHILWELL EXPLOSION, ORCHARD COTTAGE
1ST JULY 1918

Shortly after 7pm on Monday 1st July 1918, a catastrophic explosion occurred at the No 6 Shell Filling Factory, Chilwell – the biggest civilian tragedy of WW1. 139 civilian workers were killed and some 250 injured, many severely and the majority of those killed were never identified. Despite the sheer scale of the disaster, which damaged buildings up to a mile away, production resumed within a few days.

THE CHILWELL
EXPLOSION
1st JULY 1918
Killed 139 people at the nearby
No.6 Shell Filling Factory
ALBERT HALL
Chief Engineer, a survivor
lived here

Shell production, 1916-1918, courtesy of Paula Hammond

Under the direction of Viscount Chetwynd, the factory had been built quickly to meet the urgent need for more high explosive shells, and started production in early 1916. By the end of the war it had filled more than half of all the high explosive ordnance produced in Great Britain during WW1.

On Sunday 1st July 2012 two plaques were unveiled to commemorate the explosion and those killed. Plaque 24 is on the gable wall of Orchard Cottage, Chetwynd Road, Chilwell, formerly the main road from Chilwell to Long Eaton until the road was severed when building work started in 1915.

Dating from about 1895, Orchard Cottage was around 200 yards from the seat of the explosion and was severely damaged in the blast. By then it was the home of Albert Hall, Engineer-in-Charge of Experimental Work. Albert survived, but his son Geoffrey, aged thirteen, who was playing outside, was injured. Albert died in February 1941 in a car accident.

62 Chetwynd Road, Chilwell, NG9 5GD
NGR: SK 5109 3528
Plaque unveiled 1st July 2012

Albert Hall in later life

THE CHILWELL EXPLOSION, MASS GRAVES
1st July 1918

This second plaque is in St Mary's Churchyard, Attenborough, and stands adjacent to three mass graves containing the remains of many of those killed. The church burial register indicates that it was not known exactly how many individuals were buried in each coffin. Only thirty-two of the total killed were positively identified, four of whom are in these Attenborough graves, others elsewhere. A timber memorial erected shortly after the event disappeared in the 1970s.

THE CHILWELL EXPLOSION

On 1st July 1918 an explosion destroyed part of the Chilwell Shell Filling Factory killing 139 workers.

Many of the victims are buried in these graves.

Aftermath of the Chilwell Explosion

After WW1 the Shell Filling Factory became an army depot that later played a significant part in WW2 as Chilwell Ordnance Depot, now Chetwynd Barracks. In the grounds, close to the seat of the explosion, stands the 1919 memorial listing the names of all those killed, plus two men who died in a smaller explosion in 1917.

In a glass jar buried inside the Memorial is an account of the explosion, written by Geoffrey Hall, '... *I was in the garden and saw a great black mass coming towards me. The ground shuddered and I tried to run and was flying through the air. I was in hospital for 7 weeks.*'

Churchyard of St Mary
the Virgin, Church Lane,
Attenborough, NG9 6AS

NGR: SK 5191 3431

Plaque unveiled 1st July 2012

Chetwynd Barracks Memorial, courtesy of Alan Dance

ATTENBOROUGH STATION WAR MEMORIAL

Not strictly a blue plaque, but included in the Plaque Scheme as otherwise the memorial would have been lost.

The memorial itself is a replica of the original engraved marble tablet paid for by public subscription. It stood for many years on the Nottingham-bound platform at Attenborough Station to commemorate six staff killed in action in WW1. The replica closely matches the shape and size of the original with identical wording, but carved in black granite rather than white marble.

Original memorial, courtesy of Alan Dance

The original suffered vandalism in the 1970s. It was eventually repaired and re-erected before sustaining further irreparable damage in 2011.

Munitions Workers, 1918, courtesy of Nottingham City Council and www.picturethepast.org.uk

Early 20th century railways were far more labour-intensive than now, as indicated by the six men commemorated. Attenborough Station was well used by many thousands of munitions workers employed at the Shell Filling Factory during WW1. A footbridge was provided, and to accommodate extra long trains the platforms were extended. These have since been cut back and the station buildings have also gone.

Station Footbridge,
Attenborough Lane,
Attenborough, NG9 6AL
NGR: SK 5179 3458
Plaque unveiled 11th November 2013

REPLICA OF THE ORIGINAL,
NOW DAMAGED, MEMORIAL
REPLACED IN 2013
BY THE SOUTHERN BROXTOWE
BLUE PLAQUE GROUP
WITH FUNDING FROM
THE RAILWAY HERITAGE TRUST

Acknowledgement plaque

GENERAL HENRY IRETON
1611-1651

A principal player in the English Civil War, Henry Ireton was born at Ireton House, Attenborough, a Grade II listed former farmhouse, in the Attenborough Village Conservation Area.

General HENRY IRETON
Lawyer, confederate and son-in-law of Oliver Cromwell born here 1611 died Limerick 1651

The son of puritan parents who were prosecuted for their beliefs, he trained as a lawyer and, when King Charles I raised his standard at Nottingham in 1642 to gather an army to attack Westminster, Henry Ireton sided with Parliament. He married Oliver Cromwell's daughter Bridget in 1646, and became his right-hand man, engaging in many battles, including Marston Moor and Naseby. After Charles's defeat and trial for treason, Ireton was a signatory to the King's death warrant, with the execution following in January 1649.

Ireton House and Attenborough Church, 1910

Ireton joined Cromwell's Ireland campaign in 1649 and was left in command when Cromwell returned to England in 1650. The following year Ireton besieged Limerick, then captured it, but shortly afterwards he died there of the plague. He was given a state funeral at Westminster Abbey, but did not rest there for long. After the 1660 restoration of the monarchy, Charles II's government had Ireton's body exhumed and hung in chains.

Ireton House was also the birthplace of Henry's younger brother John (1615-1689). He became a London merchant and was knighted by Cromwell; in 1658 he was Lord Mayor of London.

15 Church Lane, Attenborough, NG9 6AS
NGR: SK 5180 3430
Plaque fixed 22nd June 2011

Henry Ireton

MANOR FARM

The sandstone post next to the plaque, at the entrance to what is now Toton Manor Farm Recreation Ground, is the only visible fragment of the medieval Toton Manor House. Possibly a gatepost, it is one of a pair that at one time could have been boundary markers. The second was lost in the 1950s.

Gatepost from
MANOR FARM
cleared c.1952

Near the sites of
TOTON WATERMILL
recorded in Domesday Book
and the medieval
MANOR HOUSE

Archaeological investigations in 2014 showed traces of a medieval tiled building superseded by Tudor, Georgian and Victorian features.

Toton Manor Farm, early 1950s, courtesy of Norman Lewis

Until the early 20th century, Toton was an agricultural community associated with the Greys of Codnor Castle (1208-1561), the Stanhopes of Elvaston Castle (1571-1653), the Warrens of Stapleford (1653-1855) and the Birkins (1855-1921), some as Lords of the Manor.

In the 18th century, a farmhouse was built on the site of the Manor House, known latterly as Jeffery's Farm, and this was cleared in the early 1950s to make way for the recreation ground.

Toton Watermill, first recorded in the *Domesday Book* and excavated in 2014, also stood near this site. Milling activities continued here until around 1906, but no traces remain now.

Manor Farm Recreation Ground, High Road, Toton, NG9 6EL

NGR: SK 5039 3429

Plaque unveiled 29th April 2014

Toton excavations, 2014

ADMIRAL SIR JOHN BORLASE WARREN, BART, GCB
1753-1822

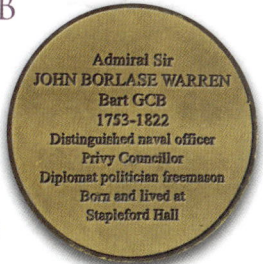

Admiral Sir
JOHN BORLASE WARREN
Bart GCB
1753-1822
Distinguished naval officer
Privy Councillor
Diplomat politician freemason
Born and lived at
Stapleford Hall

He was a great naval officer who served his country well, a popular local hero. *'Warren for ever!'* cried local crowds at the news of Sir John's triumphs at sea.

John Borlase Warren was born and lived at Stapleford Hall, a stone's throw from the plaque. He enjoyed a distinguished naval career, rising from able seaman in 1771 to Admiral in 1810. Many successes in the Channel and off the French coast led to him being honoured in 1794 as a Knight Companion of the Order of the Bath (KB) and being granted the freedom of Nottingham. In 1796 his squadron captured or destroyed some 220 French vessels. In 1798 the thwarting of a French fleet from aiding an Irish rebellion against Britain earned him the thanks of Parliament and the freedom of London and Londonderry.

Stapleford Hall

As a politician, he was MP for Great Marlow, for Nottingham and then for Buckingham. He was sworn in as a Privy Councillor in 1802 and appointed Ambassador to the Russian Court at St Petersburg from 1802-1804.

He returned to sea as Commander-in-Chief of the fleet off North America from 1807-1810 and again in 1813-1814, first fighting the French and then the Americans. In 1815 he was elevated to the Knight Grand Cross of the Order of the Bath (GCB).

Walter Parker VC Memorial Square, near 71 Derby Road, Stapleford, NG9 7AR
NGR: SK 4869 3701
Plaque unveiled 18th May 2011

Admiral Sir John Borlase Warren, Bart, GCB

ARTHUR HENRY MEE
1875-1943

Arthur Mee made a unique contribution to popular education in the first half of the 20th century. Born in a cottage (since demolished), close to St Helen's Church, Stapleford, he attended the local boys' school (now the Arthur Mee Centre and part of the Church Street, Stapleford Conservation Area), where his insatiable desire for learning was fostered by the headmaster.

ARTHUR HENRY MEE
1875-1943
Journalist and prolific author
Originator and editor of
The Children's Encyclopedia,
The Children's Newspaper and
The King's England
Born in Stapleford and
attended school here

Some Arthur Mee publications, courtesy of Alan Clayton

At fourteen he started work with the local press by being articled to the *Nottingham Daily Express* and by twenty he was editor of the *Nottingham Evening News*. He moved to London and worked on the magazine *Titbits*, eventually becoming literary editor of the *Daily Mail*.

In response to his daughter's intense curiosity, he published the *Children's Encyclopedia* in fortnightly issues from 1908, followed by a set of bound volumes. In 1919 he started the weekly *Children's Newspaper*, which soon reached a circulation of half a million and was sold all over the English speaking world. He was a prolific author and editor of many books, several for children. His last major series, *The King's England*, included a volume on each county. Some of his works remain in demand to this day.

Arthur Mee Centre, Church Street, Stapleford, NG9 8GA
NGR: SK 4888 3724
Plaque unveiled 22nd March 2011

Portrait by Frank O Salisbury, courtesy of Stapleford Library

WESLEY PLACE METHODIST CHAPEL

John Wesley (1703-1791), the great founder of Methodism, preached near here almost 250 years ago. He records in his journal for 27th March 1774: *'Sunday about noon, I preached at Stapleford six miles from Nottingham. I stood in a meadow, because no house could contain the congregation.'*

> **WESLEY PLACE METHODIST CHAPEL**
> Built in 1782 near the spot where
> **JOHN WESLEY**
> preached in 1774 and 1780
> Enlarged 1848
> Closed for worship 1975

While travelling from Derby to Nottingham on 5th July 1780, Wesley was stopped by Stapleford people and invited into their preaching house, a small, low building. He recorded in his journal: *'The house was soon filled, and we spent half-an-hour together to our mutual comfort.'*

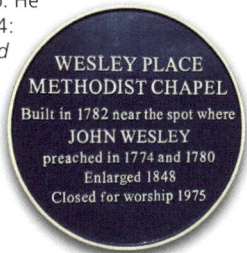

Wesley Place in 1848

The Wesley Place Chapel was built nearby in 1782 as a small, single-storey structure. Various additions were made over subsequent years through to 1883, including side bays and an upper gallery. It finally closed for worship in 1975, immediately prior to the opening of Stapleford's Eatons Road Methodist Church in January 1976. For over 100 years the building has been used as a convenient meeting place for many other organisations and now has Grade II listed status.

Stapleford House, Wesley Place, Stapleford, NG9 8DP
NGR: SK 4922 3742
Plaque unveiled 17th June 2013

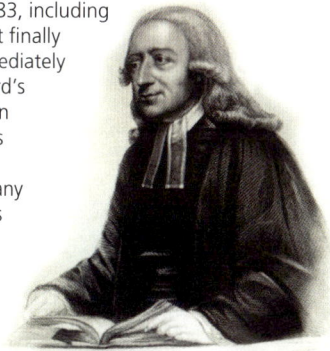

ST JOHN'S C OF E PRIMARY SCHOOL

This school is the second oldest in Nottinghamshire still in its original building, now Grade II listed. In 2013 it completed a period of refurbishment, requiring the school to vacate its premises for six months, but returning in time to celebrate the end of its 175th year.

ST JOHN'S CHURCH OF ENGLAND (VOLUNTARY CONTROLLED) PRIMARY SCHOOL
Founded and endowed in 1837 by Dame Caroline Warren of Stapleford Hall

Church schools are usually named after the patron saint of the local parish church, i.e. St Helen's, but Dame Caroline Warren of Stapleford Hall (widow of Admiral Sir John Borlase Warren), who founded and endowed the school in 1837, insisted that it should be named after her deceased husband **(plaque 29)**.

St John's C of E Primary School, courtesy of Nigel Brooks

A notable headmaster was Cecil Rollin Vickers from 1904 to 1943, interrupted only by WW1, when he served in the Royal Navy in the Middle and Far East, at one time alongside T E Lawrence (of Arabia). He was prominent in the community, with interests in welfare and especially with the Church, being a founder member of St Andrew's Mission Church Building Committee and several other organisations. He was a St Helen's churchwarden from 1913 to 1932, continuing this role in an honorary capacity, and he is immortalised by an inscription on the foundation stone of the WW1 Memorial Chapel.

80 Nottingham Road, Stapleford, NG9 8AQ
NGR: SK 4930 3744
Plaque unveiled 14th June 2013

Borlase Warren Coat of Arms, courtesy of Nigel Brooks

FREDERIC CHATFIELD SMITH, MP
1823-1905

Still remembered locally as 'Banker Smith', he was a descendant of the Smith banking family, founders of the first English regional bank in the 1680s. He joined the bank and ultimately rose to become senior partner. The premises in Nottingham survive as a NatWest branch on South Parade.

FREDERIC
CHATFIELD SMITH MP
1823 - 1905
Smith's Bank, South Parade
Nottingham
lived at
BRAMCOTE HALL
demolished 1969

An exceptional man, he was described as shrewd, clear-headed and cultured. He was MP for North Nottinghamshire from 1868-1880, a JP, a Deputy Lieutenant of Nottinghamshire, High Sheriff of Nottinghamshire for 1874 and an early president of Notts. County Football Club – even an occasional player and team captain. A man of faith, he became the patron of the Church of St Michael and All Angels, Bramcote, in 1875 and funded the building of Christ Church, Chilwell.

Bramcote Hall, 1908

In 1858 he married Harriet Matilda Pym and they had eleven surviving children. They moved into Bramcote Hall in the mid-1860s, subsequently extending it to accommodate their large family. His widow continued to live there until her death in 1914, the family selling the estate in 1920. In 1921 it became a preparatory school for Trent College, Long Eaton, but relocated in 1965 when the Hall and grounds were sold to the University of Nottingham. Bramcote Hall was demolished in 1969. The site is within the Bramcote Conservation Area.

Moss Drive, Bramcote, NG9 3NF
NGR: SK 5080 3748
Plaque unveiled 24th April 2013

Portrait, 1877, courtesy of Val Bird

HENRY JOHN PEARSON
1850-1913

Two members of the Pearson family - father and son - are commemorated on this plaque.

Henry John Pearson, great-grandson of Chilwell nurseryman John Pearson **(plaque 20)**, joined with Robert Foster as Foster and Pearson to manufacture glasshouses, before founding, in 1893, with younger brother Louis Frederick **(plaque 5)**, the Beeston Foundry Company and becoming its first chairman. Later, the firm became the Beeston Boiler Company, a major Beeston employer.

HENRY
JOHN PEARSON
1850 - 1913
Co-founder of Beeston Foundry Co
later Beeston Boiler Co
a noted ornithologist, and his son
Lt Colonel NOEL GERVIS
PEARSON DSO MC
1884 - 1958
both local philanthropists
lived here

Beeston Boiler Works, courtesy of J M Jones and www.picturethepast.org.uk and Foster and Pearson brass casting, c.1870-90

He lived in Broadgate, Beeston, married Laura Kate Rogers in 1877 and in the late 1880s moved to The White House in Town Street, Bramcote. They had seven children including Stephen Hetley **(plaque 13)** and Noel Gervis (page opposite).

Henry John had a life-long interest away from industry as a noted ornithologist, making several expeditions to Arctic regions and publishing many papers on bird life. He was a Fellow of the British Ornithological, Royal Geographical and Royal Horticultural Societies. Locally he was the principal donor behind Dovecote Lane Recreation Ground, and on the committees of Nottingham Convalescent Homes and Hospital for Women. He died in Egypt in 1913 and is buried at St Mary's Church, Attenborough. There is a memorial to him in the Church of St Michael and All Angels, Bramcote.

White House, Town Street, Bramcote, NG9 3DP
NGR: SK 5088 3743
Plaque unveiled 18th April 2013

Henry John Pearson

LT. COL. NOEL GERVIS PEARSON, DSO, MC
1884-1958

The White House, 1965, courtesy of J Orton and www.picturethepast.org.uk

Another of the Pearsons who continued the family tradition of industry, service and philanthropy, was Beeston-born Noel Gervis, the youngest son of Henry John Pearson (opposite page) and youngest brother of Stephen Hetley Pearson **(plaque 13)**. He married Kathleen Mary Nicholls in 1914 and moved into The White House, Town Street, Bramcote. They had four sons and two daughters.

During WW1 he saw active service on the Western Front and was awarded the MC in 1916 and DSO in 1918. Sadly, two of his sons were killed in action in WW2. He was High Sheriff for Nottinghamshire for 1935 and became chairman of Beeston Boiler Company in 1943. He was well known for his philanthropic work with local churches and was very closely associated with the Nottingham hospitals as president or chairman of the Children's Hospital, General Hospital and General Dispensary.

Noel Gervis was County Commissioner for the Boy Scouts, and facilitated the acquisition of Walesby Park by the Nottinghamshire Scouts. He was also President of the Beeston Branch of the Royal British Legion and the President of the Beeston Boys' Brigade. The White House, where he died, is in the Bramcote Conservation Area.

White House, Town Street, Bramcote, NG9 3DP
NGR: SK 5088 3743
Plaque unveiled 18th April 2013

Lt. Col. Noel Gervis Pearson

ACKNOWLEDGEMENTS

The Group gratefully acknowledges the goodwill, support, encouragement and sponsorship of all those who have contributed in so many ways to the success of this project.

We thank the many individuals and organisations who have participated directly in the essential historical research. In addition to the members of the Group, and other members of the four local societies represented by the Group, we would particularly like to thank English Heritage and Professor John Beckett for guidance and advice, David Hallam, Gillian Morral and the late Margaret Cooper.

Additionally, we have been helped in many other ways, including more general support and advice; by those who have willingly allowed plaques to be fixed to their properties; by others contributing to unveiling ceremonies through hospitality, catering and publicity, and through generous donations that have allowed each plaque to be self-financed. The diversity of participants has been wide-ranging, with support from property owners, local businesses, schools, church authorities, families and descendants of those celebrated.

For plaque funding we thank many individuals and others for generous financial support, including the Railway Heritage Trust, Network Rail, and the participating societies. Leander Architectural was most helpful with plaque design and fixing.

We thank all those involved in unveilings, particularly Broxtowe Borough Council and Stapleford Town Council and their mayors, councillors and officers and other elected representatives, Church authorities, the military, Lincolnshire and Nottinghamshire Air Ambulance and the many personalities who have given their time freely at unveilings, including Sir Neil Cossons, Sir Paul Smith, Sir William McAlpine, Judy Loe and Kate Beckinsale. For press coverage we thank the *Nottingham Post, Bygones, Beeston Express* and *The Beestonian*.

Finally, we thank all involved in the production of this Guide, including those outside the Group who have supplied images, our proofreaders, those who have checked National Grid References and our designer Jonathan Tait. We have tried to acknowledge images accurately and we apologise for any that are inaccurately attributed or inadvertently unattributed.

GUIDE SPONSORSHIP

This Guide has been financed by the generosity of the Beeston and District Civic Society, the Stapleford & District Local History Society, the former Beeston BID, G. H. Hurt & Son Ltd., Leander Architectural, Tramlink Nottingham Ltd. (trading as NET), C P Walker & Son, Bartons plc and Jonathan Tait Design.

In addition we have received two generous anonymous donations. All of this support is gratefully acknowledged.

LEANDER
ARCHITECTURAL

G.H.HURT & SON
NOTTINGHAM, SINCE 1912

BARTONS

C P Walker & Son

BEESTONBID
Your Beeston Your Future

NET
NOTTINGHAM EXPRESS TRANSIT

Beeston
AND DISTRICT
Civic
Society

Stapleford
and District
Local History
Society

Jonathan Tait
FREELANCE DESIGN

Beeston AND DISTRICT Civic Society

PROTECTING AND IMPROVING THE ENVIRONMENT

The Society is a Registered Charity founded in 1973, now with some 230 members. In more than forty years we have supported better public services, campaigned for conservation areas, saved buildings, planted trees and taken part in public enquiries.

Strictly non-political our aims are:

- To make Beeston and District a better place for all who live, work, shop and visit;

- To protect the best of our physical environment and promote high standards of architecture, design and planning; and

- To eliminate eyesores and areas of neglect within our community.

The future of Beeston and District can benefit from your interest, your time and your support. Join us in raising an awareness of our surroundings through discussion, guided walks and the Annual Heritage Open Days. Together we can make a difference.

For more information see: www.beestoncivicsociety.org.uk
For more details contact: beestoncivicsociety@gmail.com

Beeston & District Local History Society

Founded 1972

The Society's aims and objectives are the study and promotion of the history of the area, the recording of present developments, and the collection and conservation of documents, photographs and artefacts as the Society considers relevant.

The Society meets on the third Wednesday each month through the year at the Chilwell Memorial Institute, High Road, Chilwell. Doors open at 7.10 pm and meetings start at 7.30 pm. A programme of topics on both local and general history is presented by a variety of speakers.

The Society maintains an expanding and important archive of local material which is available for research by members and is used at Society and public displays, including the Heritage Open Days and Beeston Carnival. A local history library is available on request at meetings.

Visitors and new members always welcome.

For more information see: www.beestonhistory.org.uk

Stapleford and District Local History Society

Stapleford and District Local History Society was founded in 1995 to promote interest in and awareness of the history of the local area. The Society meets on the second Tuesday monthly (with the exception of January and August) at St. Helen's Church Hall on Frederick Road. Doors open at 7.00pm and an illustrated presentation by a speaker follows notices at 7.30pm.

We have a large lending library of books on the local and Nottinghamshire area. A sales stall offers cards, tea towels, books etc with a Stapleford theme.

The Society preserves records, documents and photographs, and an active archives group keeps them in good order.

Our two most recently published books *Stapleford in World War Two* and *Stapleford Past and Present* are available for sale at Stapleford library.

Visitors and new members are always welcome. Come along and give us a try.

For more information see: www.staplefordlocalhistory.co.uk

The Society was formed in 1971 with the aim of monitoring the care and preservation of buildings of historic and architectural interest within the designated conservation area and its surroundings, in which there are eleven listed sites, and to oppose any unnecessary development proposals which could be detrimental to the ethos of the area.

The Society also maintains a watching brief over any potential damage to the environment, to woodland and to wildlife.

The Society arranges two events during the year with a speaker, usually in the spring and autumn, and the Annual General Meeting is held in June.

For more information see: www.bramcoteconservation.org.uk

STAPLEFORD

CHURCH STREET

30

DERBY ROAD

29 P

P

31

32

NOTTINGHAM RO

BRIAN CLOUGH WAY

A52

TOTON LANE

TRAM

P

To ◄
Derby
M1 J25

STAPLEFORD LANE

TOTON

HIGH RD

P 28

NOTTINGHAM RO

◄ Long Eaton

ATTENBOROUGH

NATURE RESERVE

P

27

25

RIVER TRENT

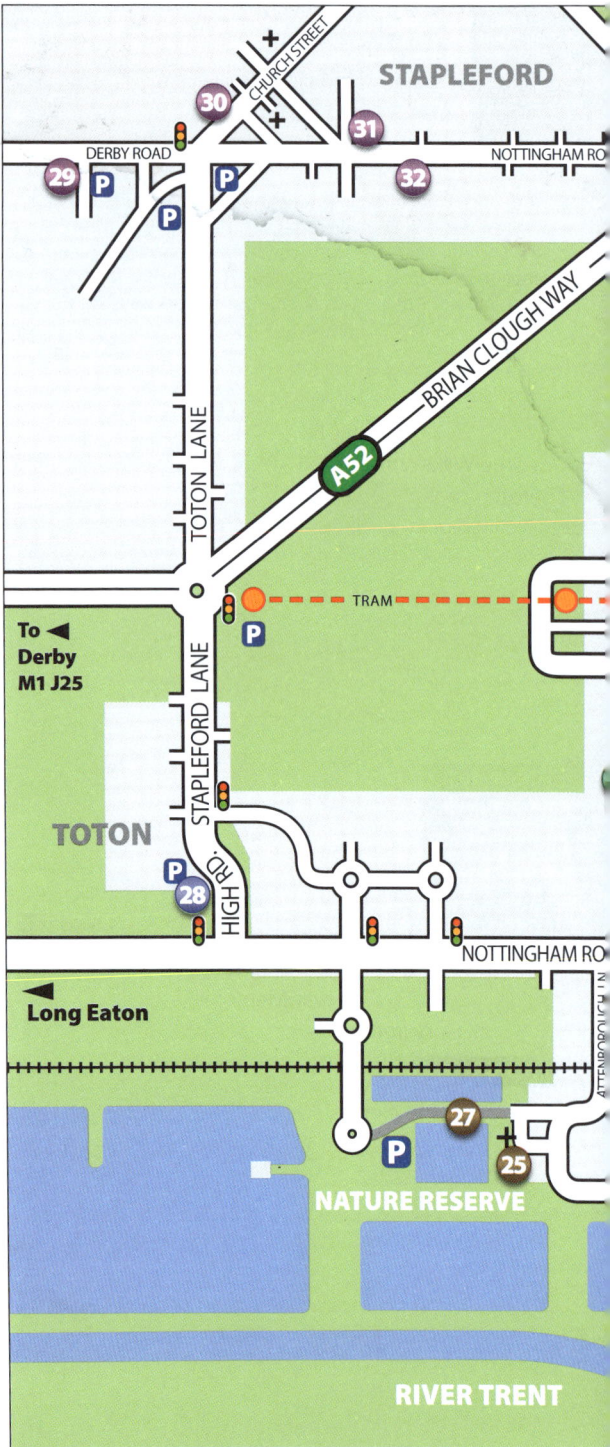

Please note: not all minor roads shown. Not to scale

BLUE PLAQUE KEY

Blue plaques have been with us for a hundred and fifty years, viewed with curiosity and pleasure by all who are interested in the history of people and places. The first, on a house in London, was not blue and it no longer survives, but it did have something of a Nottinghamshire connection. It marked the birthplace of Lord Byron. From that small beginning the idea has unfolded across communities all over the country.

Today, in this most imaginative of schemes, thirty-four plaques across six townships in Broxtowe link people with the buildings where they lived or worked, mark notable places or signal events important in the area's history.

Most are cause for celebration, highlighting people who, through their distinction, contributed to the life of the neighbourhood. Others mark significant buildings and two a terrible tragedy – the 1918 explosion at the Chilwell Shell Filling Factory.

For me, they are an eye-opener. Throughout my boyhood in Beeston I had little idea of the extraordinary diversity of distinguished people who are part of the area's history. These blue plaques change all that. They offer an intriguing insight into an otherwise invisible past. And, they are there for everybody - to seek out using this booklet or to discover by chance, a memorable surprise on an afternoon walk.

Neil Cossons

Designed by tait-design.com
Published on behalf of the Southern Broxtowe Blue Plaque Group by Beeston and District Civic Society
www.beestoncivicsociety.org.uk

ISBN 978-0-9510848-6-1